Packing for my Holidays

Mary O'Keeffe

GILL EDUCATION

Let's go on **holidays**!
We have a lot to pack.
This is how we do it.
Step 1: Let's get a **suitcase**.

The suitcases are empty.

Mam has a big **suitcase**.

Dad has a big **suitcase** too.

I have one that is not so big.

Step 2: We pick the bits that we need for the **holiday**.

You can bring small suitcases onto the plane with you.

It is a lot of fun to pack the bags! The **holiday** will be fun for us all!

Step 3: Mam helps me to pack. It is a big job. She puts some tops, pants and socks in a set.

Step 4: Next, we pack the fun stuff! I have my sun hat.

I have my ted in as well. He has to come on **holidays**!

I like to fill up my suitcase. Have I got all that I need for my **holidays**?

I need my sunglasses.
They are red.
I will pop them in my **suitcase**.
Next, I want to put in a big mat.

I will put it on the sand.
It will be hot.
I need **suncream** too.
I will put it on in the sun.

I need my flip-flops.
I can put them on if it gets hot.
They go in my **suitcase**.

I like to dig in the sand. I need a bucket. I will pop it in my **suitcase** too.

I have put a lot in! I will have to sit on my **suitcase**! Mam will help! It will zip up.

You can fit more in your suitcase when you roll up your clothes.

Yes! My **suitcase** is full. Let's go!

Let's have fun on **holidays**!